Philippine Folklore Stories

John Maurice Miller

Contents

PHILIPPINE FOLKLORE STORIES

STORIES

BY

John Maurice Miller

Preface

As these stories are only legends that have been handed down from remote times, the teacher must impress upon the minds of the children that they are myths and are not to be given credence; otherwise the imaginative minds of the native children would accept them as truth, and trouble would be caused that might be hard to remedy. Explain then the fiction and show the children the folly of belief in such fanciful tales.

The Tobacco of Harisaboqued

A legend of the volcano of Canlaon on the island of Negros. It is told generally in Western Negros and Eastern Cebu. The volcano is still active, and smoke and steam rise from its crater.

Long before the strange men came over the water from Spain, there lived in Negros, on the mountain of Canlaon, an old man who had great power over all the things in the earth. He was called Harisaboqued, King of the Mountain.

When he wished anything done he had but to tap the ground three times and instantly a number of little men would spring from the earth to answer his call. They would obey his slightest wish, but as he was a kind old man and never told his dwarfs to do anything wrong, the people who lived near were not afraid. They planted tobacco on the mountain side and were happy and prosperous,

The fields stretched almost to the top of the mountain and the plants grew well, for every night Harisaboqued would order his dwarfs to attend to them, and though the tobacco was high up it grew faster and better than that planted in the valley below.

The people were very grateful to the old man and were willing to do anything for him; but he only asked them not to plant above a line he had ordered his little men to draw around the mountain near the top. He wished that place for himself and his dwarfs.

All obeyed his wish and no one planted over the line. It was a pretty sight to see the long rows of tobacco plants extending from the towns below far up to the line on the mountain side.

One day Harisaboqued called the people together and told them that he was going away for a long time. He asked them again not to plant over the line, and told them that if they disregarded this wish he would carry all the tobacco away and permit no more to grow on the mountain side until he had smoked what he had taken. The people promised faithfully to obey him. Then he tapped on the ground, the earth opened, and he disappeared into the mountain.

Many years passed and Harisaboqued did not come back. All wondered why he did not return and at last decided that he would never do so. The whole mountain side was covered with tobacco and many of the people looked with greedy eyes at the bare ground above the line, but as yet they were afraid to break their promise.

At last one man planted in the forbidden ground, and, as nothing happened, others did the same, until soon the mountain was entirely covered with the waving plants. The people were very happy and soon forgot about Harisaboqued and their promise to him.

But one day, while they were laughing and singing, the earth suddenly opened and Harisaboqued sprang out before them. They were very much frightened and fled in terror down the mountain side. When they reached the foot and looked back they saw a terrible sight. All the tobacco had disappeared and, instead of the thousands of plants that they had tended so carefully, nothing but the bare mountain could be seen.

Then suddenly there was a fearful noise and the whole mountain top flew high in the air, leaving an immense hole from which poured fire and smoke.

The people fled and did not stop until they were far away. Harisaboqued had kept his word.

Many years have come and gone, but the mountain is bare and the smoke still rolls out of the mountain top. Villages have sprung up along the sides, but no tobacco is grown on the mountain. The people remember the tales of the former great crops and turn longing eyes to the heights above them, but they will have to wait. Harisaboqued is still smoking his tobacco.

The Pericos

Throughout the Visayan islands almost every family owns a pericos, kept as American children keep canary birds. The pericos is about the size and color of a Crow, but has a hard white hood that entirely covers its head. The people teach it but one phrase, which it repeats continually, parrot fashion. The words are, "Comusta pari? Pericos tao." (How are you, father? Parrot-man.) "Pari" means padre or priest. The people address the pericos as "pari" because its white head, devoid of feathers, seems to resemble the shaven crowns of the friars and native priests.

I

In his small wooden box That hangs on the wall Sits a queer-looking bird That in words sounds his call. From daybreak to twilight His cry he repeats, Resting only whenever He drinks or he eats. He never grows weary,-- Hear! There he goes now! "Comusta pari? Pericos tao."

II

And all the day long You can hear this strange cry:
"How are you, father? A parrot-man I." He sits on his perch, In his little white cap, And pecks at your hand If the cage door you tap. Now give him some seeds, Hear him say with a bow, "Comusta pari? Pericos tao."

III

Poor little birdie! How hard it must be To sit there in prison And never be free! I'll give you a mango, And teach you to say "Thank you," and "Yes, sir," And also "Good day." You'll find English as easy As what you say now, "Comusta pari? Pericos tao."

IV

I'll teach you "Good morning" And "How do you do?" Or "I am well, thank you," And "How are you too?" "Polly is hungry" or "It's a fine day." These and much more I am sure you could say. But now I must go, So say with your bow, "Comusta pari? Pericos tao."

Quicoy and the Ongloc

This story is known generally in the southern Islands. The Ongloc is feared by the children just as some little boys and girls fear the Bogy Man. The tale is a favorite one among the children and they believe firmly in the fate of Quicoy.

Little Quicoy's name was Francisco, but every one called him Quicoy, which, in Visayan, is the pet name for Francisco. He was a good little boy and helped his mother grind the corn and pound the rice in the big wooden bowl, but one night he was very careless. While playing in the corner with the cat he upset the jar of lubi lana, and all the oil ran down between the bamboo strips in the floor and was lost. There was none left to put in the glass and light, so the whole family had to go to bed in the dark.

Quicoy's mother was angry. She whipped him with her chinela and then opened the window and cried:

"Ongloc of the mountains! Fly in through the door. Catch Quicoy and eat him, He is mine no more."

Quicoy was badly frightened when he heard this, for the Ongloc is a big black man with terrible long teeth, who all night goes searching for the bad boys and girls that he may change them into little cocoanuts and put them on a shelf in his rock house in the mountains to eat when he is hungry.

So when Quicoy went to his bed in the corner he pulled the matting over his head and was so afraid that he did not go to sleep for a long time.

The next morning he rose very early and went down to the spring where the boys get the water to put in the bamboo poles and carry home. Some boys were already there, and he told them what had taken place the night before. They were all sorry that his mother had called the Ongloc, but they told him not to be afraid for they would tell him how he could be forever safe from that terrible man.

It was very easy. All he had to do was to go at dusk to the cocoanut grove by the river and dig holes under two trees. Then he was to climb a tree, get the cocoanut that grew the highest, and, after taking off the husk and punching in one of the little eyes, whisper inside:

"Ongloc of the mountains! Ongloc! Ugly man! I'm a little cocoanut, Catch me if you can!"

Then he was to cut the cocoanut in halves, quickly bury one piece in one of the holes, and, running to the other tree, bury the remaining half in the other hole. After that he might walk home safely, being sure not to run, for the Ongloc has always to obey the call of the cocoanut, and must hunt through the grove to find the one that called him. Should he cross the line between the holes, the buried pieces would fly out of the holes, snap together on him, and, flying up the tree from which they came, would keep him prisoner for a hundred years.

Quicoy was happy to think that he could capture the Ongloc, and resolved to go that very night. He wanted some of the boys to go with him, but they said he must go alone or the charm would be broken. They also told him to be careful himself and not cross the line between the holes or he would be caught as easily as the Ongloc.

So Quicoy went home and kept very quiet all day. His mother was sorry she had frightened him the night before, and was going to tell him not to be afraid; but when she thought of the lubi lana spilled on the ground, she resolved to punish him more by saying nothing to him.

Just at dark, when no one was looking, Quicoy took his father's bolo and quietly slipped away to the grove down by the river. He was not afraid of ladrones, but he needed the bolo because it is not easy to open a cocoanut, and it takes some time, even with a bolo, to get the husk chopped from the fruit.

Quicoy felt a little frightened when he saw all the big trees around him. The wind made strange noises in the branches high above him, and all the trees seemed to be leaning over and trying to speak to him. He felt somewhat sorry that he had come, but when he thought of the Ongloc he mustered up courage and went on until he found an open space between two high trees.

He stopped here and dug a hole under each of the trees. Then he put his feet in the notches and climbed one of the trees. It was hard work, for the notches were far apart; but at last he reached the branches and climbed to the top. The wind rocked the tree and made him dizzy, but he reached the highest cocoanut, threw it to the ground, and then 'started down the tree. It was easy to come down, though he went too fast and slipped and slid some distance, skinning his arms and legs. He did not mind that, however, for he knew he had the cocoanut that would capture the Ongloc. He picked it up, chopped off the husk, punched in one of the little eyes, and whispered inside:

"Ongloc of the mountains! Ongloc! Ugly man! I'm a little cocoanut, Catch me if you can!"

He then chopped it in halves and buried one piece, and, running to the other tree, buried the remaining piece. Just as he finished he thought he heard a noise in the grove, and, instead of walking, he started to run as fast as he could.

It was very dark now, and the noise grew louder and made him run faster and faster, until suddenly a dreadful scream sounded directly in front of him, and a terrible black thing with fiery eyes came flying at him. He turned in terror and ran back toward the trees. He knew it was the Ongloc answering the call of the cocoanut, and he ran like mad, but the monster had seen him and flew after him, screaming with rage.

Faster and faster he ran, but nearer and nearer sounded the frightful screams until, just as he felt two huge claws close on his neck, there was a bump, a loud snap, and he felt himself being carried high in the air. When the shock was over he found that he was squeezed tightly between two hard walls, and he could hear the Ongloc screaming and tearing at the outside with his claws. Then he knew what had happened.

He had crossed the line between the buried pieces and they had snapped on him and carried him up the tree from which they came. He was badly squeezed but he felt safe from the Ongloc, who finally went away in disappointment; for, although he likes cocoanuts, he cannot take one from a tree, but must change a boy or girl into the fruit if he wishes to eat of it.

Quicoy waited a long, long time and then knocked on the shell in the hope that some one would hear him. All that night and the next day and the next he knocked and cried and knocked, but, though people passed under the tree and found the bolo, he was so high up they did not hear him.

Days and weeks went by and the people wondered what had become of Quicoy. Many thought he had run away and were sorry for his poor mother, who grieved very much to think she had terrified him by calling the Ongloc. Of course the boys who had sent him to the grove could have told something of his whereabouts, but they were frightened and said nothing, so no one ever heard of poor little Quicoy again.

If you pass a cocoanut grove at night you can hear a noise like some one knocking. The older people say that the cocoanuts grow so closely together high up in the branches that the wind, when it shakes the tree, bumps them together. But the children know better. They say, "Quicoy is knocking to get out, but he must stay there a hundred years."

The Passing of Loku

The tale of Loku is applied to a large, ugly lizard which climbs to the rafters of houses and gives the peculiar cry that suggests its name. This lizard, although hideous, is harmless; it lives on centipedes. Its strange cry may be heard everywhere in the Philippine Islands.

Hundreds of years ago a very wicked king named Loku ruled the Philippines. He was cruel and unjust, and condemned to death all who refused to do his bidding. He had vast armies and made war on all until his name was feared everywhere.

His power was very great. He conquered every nation that opposed him and killed so many people that the god, viewing the slaughter from his throne above, sent an angel to order him to cease from warfare and to rule the land in peace.

Loku was in his palace, planning an assault on his neighbors, when a soft light filled the chamber, and a beautiful angel appeared and delivered the mandate of the master.

The cruel king paid no heed, but dismissed the holy messenger in scorn. "Tell your master," said he, "to deliver his message in person. I do not deal with messengers. I am Loku. All fear my name. I am the great Loku."

Hardly had he spoken when the palace shook to its foundations and a mighty voice thundered, "Is it thus thou slightest my word? Thou art Loku. All shall indeed know thy name. From every crevice thou shalt forever cry it in a form that suits thy ill nature."

The courtiers, alarmed by the shock, rushed to the king's chamber, but Loku was nowhere to be found. The royal robes lay scattered on the floor and the only living thing to be seen was an ugly lizard that blinked at them from among the plans on the table.

They searched far and wide, and when no trace of the king could be found the courtiers divided the kingdom and ruled so wisely and well that there was peace for many years.

As for Loku, you may still hear him fulfilling his punishment. From crack and crevice, tree and shrub, he calls his name from dark till dawn: "Lok-u! Lok-u! Lok-u!"

And he must cry it forever.

The Light of the Fly

The firefly abounds everywhere in the Islands.

I

The King of the Air was in terrible rage, For some one had stolen his ring; And every one wondered whoever could dare To do such a terrible thing. He called all his subjects together and said, "To him that shall find it I'll give Whatever he asks, and this bounty of mine Shall last while his family live."

II

Away went his good loyal subjects to search, And no one remained but a fly. "Be off!" said the King, "go and join in the search; Would you slight such a ruler as I?" Then up spoke the fly with his little wee voice: "The ring is not stolen," he said. "It stuck to your crown when you put it away, And now it's on top of your head."

III

The King in surprise took the crown from his head, And there, sure enough, was the ring. "No wonder you saw it, with so many eyes; But what is your wish?" said the King. "O King," said the fly, "I work hard all the day, And I never can go out at night. I should like to go then and be gay with my friends, So all that I wish is a light."

IV

"You shall have it at once," said the gratified King, And he fastened a light to the fly, Who straightway returned to his home with the prize That was worth more than money could buy. So now you can see him at night with his light And from him this lesson may learn: To keep your eyes open and see the least thing, And Fortune will come in its turn.

Mangita and Larina

This is a tale told in the lake district of Luzon. At times of rain or in winter the waters of the Laguna de Bai rise and detach from the banks a peculiar vegetation that resembles lettuce. These plants, which float for months down the Pasig River, gave rise, no doubt, to the story.

Many years ago there lived on the banks of the Laguna de Bai a poor fisherman whose wife had died, leaving him two beautiful daughters named Mangita and Larina.

Mangita had hair as black as night and a dark skin. She was as good as she was beautiful, and was loved by all for her kindness. She helped her father mend the nets and make the torches to fish with at night, and her bright smile lit up the little nipa house like a ray of sunshine.

Larina was fair and had long golden hair of which she was very proud. She was different from her sister, and never helped with the work, but spent the day combing her hair and catching butterflies. She would catch a pretty butterfly, cruelly stick a pin through it, and fasten it in her hair. Then she would go down to the lake to see her reflection in the clear water, and would laugh to see the poor butterfly struggling in pain. The people disliked her for her cruelty, but they loved Mangita very much. This made Larina jealous, and the more Mangita was loved, the more her sister thought evil of her.

One day a poor old woman came to the nipa house and begged for a little rice to put in her bowl. Mangita was mending a net and Larina was combing her hair in the doorway. When Larina saw the old woman she spoke mockingly to her and gave her a push that made her fall and cut her head on a sharp rock; but Mangita sprang to help her, washed the blood away from her head, and filled her bowl with rice from the jar in the kitchen.

The poor woman thanked her and promised never to forget her kindness, but to her sister she spoke not a word. Larina did not care, however, but laughed at her and mocked her as she painfully made her way again down the road. When she had gone Mangita took Larina to task for her cruel treatment of a stranger; but, instead of doing any good, it only caused Larina to hate her sister all the more.

Some time afterwards the poor fisherman died. He had gone to the big city down the river to sell his fish, and had been attacked with a terrible sickness that was raging there.

The girls were now alone in the world.

Mangita carved pretty shells and earned enough to buy food, but, though she begged Larina to try to help, her sister would only idle away the time.

The terrible sickness now swept everywhere and poor Mangita, too, fell ill. She asked Larina to nurse her, but the latter was jealous of her and would do nothing to ease her pain. Mangita grew worse and worse, but finally, when it seemed as if she would soon die, the door opened and the old woman to whom she had been so kind came into the room. She had a bag of seeds in her hand, and taking one she gave it to Mangita, who soon showed signs of being better, but was so weak that she could not give thanks.

The old woman then gave the bag to Larina and told her to give a seed to her sister every hour until she returned. She then went away and left the girls alone.

Larina watched her sister, but did not give her a single seed. Instead, she hid them in her own long hair and paid no attention to Mangita's moans of pain.

The poor girl's cries grew weaker and weaker, but not a seed would her cruel sister give her. In fact, Larina was so jealous that she wished her sister to die.

When at last the old woman returned, poor Mangita was at the point of death. The visitor bent over the sick girl and then asked her sister if she had given Mangita the seeds. Larina showed her the empty bag and said she had given them as directed. The old woman searched the house, but of course could not find the seeds. She then asked Larina again if she had given them to Mangita. Again the cruel girl said that she had done so.

Suddenly the room was filled with a blinding light, and when Larina could see once more, in place of the old woman stood a beautiful fairy holding the now well Mangita in her arms.

She pointed to Larina and said, "I am the poor woman who asked for rice. I wished to know your hearts. You were cruel and Mangita was kind, so she shall live with me in my island home in the lake. As for you, because you tried to do evil to your good sister, you shall sit at the bottom of the lake forever, combing out the seeds you have hidden in your hair." Then, she clapped her hands and a number of elves appeared and carried the struggling Larina away.

"Come," said the fairy to Mangita, and she carried her to her beautiful home, where she lives in peace and happiness.

As for Larina, she sits at the bottom of the lake and combs her hair. As she combs a seed out, another comes in, and every seed that is combed out becomes a green plant that floats out of the lake and down the Pasig.

And to this day people can see them, and know that Larina is being punished for her wickedness.

How the World Was Made

This is the ancient Filipino account of the creation.

Thousands of years ago there was no land nor sun nor moon nor stars, and the world was only a great sea of water, above which stretched the sky. The water was the kingdom of the god Maguayan, and the sky was ruled by the great god Captan.

Maguayan had a daughter called Lidagat, the sea, and Captan had a son known as Lihangin, the wind. The gods agreed to the marriage of their children, so the sea became the bride of the wind.

Three sons and a daughter were born to them. The sons were called Licalibutan, Liadlao, and Libulan, and the daughter received the name of Lisuga.

Licalibutan had a body of rock and was strong and brave; Liadlao was formed of gold and was always happy; Libulan was made of copper and was weak and timid; and the beautiful Lisuga had a body of pure silver and was sweet and gentle. Their parents were very fond of them, and nothing was wanting to make them happy.

After a time Lihangin died and left the control of the winds to his eldest son Licalibutan. The faithful wife Lidagat soon followed her husband, and the children, now grown up, were left without father or mother. However, their grandfathers, Captan and Maguayan, took care of them and guarded them from all evil.

After a time, Licalibutan, proud of his power over the winds, resolved to gain more power, and asked his brothers to join him in an attack on Captan in the sky above. At first they refused; but when Licalibutan became angry with them, the amiable Liadlao, not wishing to offend his brother, agreed to help. Then together they induced the timid Libulan to join in the plan.

When all was ready the three brothers rushed at the sky, but they could not beat down the gates of steel that guarded the entrance. Then Licalibutan let loose the strongest winds and blew the bars in every direction. The brothers rushed into the opening, but were met by the angry god Captan. So terrible did he look that they turned and ran in terror; but Captan, furious at the destruction of his gates, sent three bolts of lightning after them.

The first struck the copper Libulan and melted him into a ball. The second struck the golden Liadlao and he too was melted. The third bolt struck Licalibutan and his rocky body broke into many pieces and fell into the sea. So huge was he that parts of his body stuck out above the water and became what is known as land.

In the meantime the gentle Lisuga had missed her brothers and started to look for them. She went toward the sky, but as she approached the broken gates, Captan, blind with anger, struck her too with lightning, and her silver body broke into thousands of pieces.

Captan then came down from the sky and tore the sea apart, calling on Maguayan to come to him and accusing him of ordering the attack on the sky. Soon Maguayan appeared and answered that he knew nothing of the plot as he had been asleep far down in the sea. After a time he succeeded in calming the angry Captan. Together they wept at the loss of their grandchildren, especially the gentle and beautiful Lisuga; but with all their power they could not restore the dead to life. However, they gave to each body a beautiful light that will shine forever.

And so it was that golden Liadlao became the sun and copper Libulan the moon, while the thousands of pieces of silver Lisuga shine as the stars of heaven. To wicked Licalibutan the gods gave no light, but resolved to make his body support a new race of people. So Captan gave Maguayan a seed and he planted it on the land, which, as you will remember, was part of Licalibutan's huge body. Soon a bamboo tree grew up, and from the hollow of one of its branches a man and a woman came out. The man's name was Sicalac, and the woman was called Sicabay. They were the parents of the human race. Their first child was a son whom they called Libo; afterwards they had a daughter who was known as Saman. Pandaguan was a younger son and he had a son called Arion.

Pandaguan was very clever and invented a trap to catch fish. The very first thing he caught was a huge shark. When he brought it to land, it looked so great and fierce that he thought it was surely a god, and he at once ordered his people to worship it. Soon all gathered around and began to sing and pray to the shark. Suddenly the sky and sea opened, and the gods came out and ordered Pandaguan to throw the shark back into the sea and to worship none but them.

All were afraid except Pandaguan. He grew very bold and answered that the shark was as big as the gods, and that since he had been able to overpower it he would also be able to conquer the gods. Then Captan, hearing this, struck Pandaguan with a small thunderbolt, for he did not wish to kill him but merely to teach him a lesson. Then he and Maguayan decided to punish these people by scattering them over the earth, so they carried some to one land and some to another. Many children were afterwards born, and thus the earth became inhabited in all parts.

Pandaguan did not die. After lying on the ground for thirty days he regained his strength, but his body was blackened from the lightning, and all his descendants ever since that day have been black.

His first son, Arion, was taken north, but as he had been born before his father's punishment he did not lose his color, and all his people therefore are white.

Libo and Saman were carried south, where the hot sun scorched their bodies and caused all their descendants to be of a brown color.

A son of Saman and a daughter of Sicalac were carried east, where the land at first was so lacking in food that they were compelled to eat clay. On this account their children and their children's children have always been yellow in color.

And so the world came to be made and peopled. The sun and moon shine in the sky and the beautiful stars light up the night. All over the land, on the body of the envious Licalibutan, the children of Sicalac and Sicabay have grown great in numbers. May they live forever in peace and brotherly love!

The Silver Shower

Every night in Manila, when the bells of the city boom out the Angelus and lights begin to appear in the windows, the walks are filled with people hurrying toward the bay. In the streets hundreds of carriages, their lamps twinkling like fireflies, speed quickly by, as the cocheros urge on the little Filipino ponies. All are bound for the Luneta to hear the evening concert.

A pretty place is the Luneta, the garden spot of the city. It is laid out in elliptical form and its green lawns are covered with benches for the people. A broad driveway surrounds it and hundreds of electric lights transform the night into day.

A band stand is located at each end of the oval, and at night concerts are given by the military bands.

Thousands of people gather to listen to the music. The bright uniforms of officers and men, the white dresses of American ladies, the black mantillas of the dark-eyed senoritas, and the gayly colored camisas of the Filipino girls show that the beauty and chivalry of Manila have assembled at the concert.

The band plays many beautiful selections and finally closes with the "Star-Spangled Banner." At once every head is bared and all stand at rigid attention till the glorious old song is finished. Then the musicians disperse, the carriages drive away, and people return to their homes.

Many, however, linger on the benches or stroll along the beach, watching the water curling upon the shore. As the waves reach the land a soft light seems to spring from them and to break into thousands of tiny stars. Now and then some one idly skips a stone over the water. Where it touches, a little fountain of liquid fire springs upward, and the water ripples away in gleaming circles that, growing wider and wider, finally disappear in a flash of silvery light.

Of all the beauties of the Islands, the water of Manila Bay at night ranks among the first. And those who ask why it flashes and glows in this way are told the story of the silver shower that saved the Pasig villages from the Moro Datto Bungtao.

Hundreds of years ago messengers came hurrying from the south of Luzon with the news that the great Datto Bungtao, with many ships and men, was on his way to the island to burn the villages and carry the people away into slavery.

Then great fear came into the hearts of the people, for the fierce Datto was the terror of the eastern seas, and all the southern islands were reported captured. Nevertheless, they resolved to defend their homes and save their people from shame and slavery.

The news proved true, for the Moro chief landed a great army on the shore of the Bay of Batangas, and his fierce followers, with fire and sword, started north to lay waste the country.

For a time they drove all before them, but soon Luzon was up in arms against them and great numbers of warriors hurried southward to battle with the Moros. All tribal feeling was forgotten and Tagalos, Macabebes, Igorrotes, and Pangasinanes hurried southward in thousands.

The Moros presently found themselves checked by a large army of men determined to save their homes or to die fighting.

Near the present town of Imus, in Cavite, a battle was fought and the Moros were defeated. They then retreated southward, but great numbers of Vicoles and Tinguianes rushed up from the southern part of the island and blocked their way.

On the shore of the great Lake Bombon the final battle was fought. The Moros were killed to a man, and with great rejoicing the tribes returned north and south to their homes.

But in the meantime Bungtao had not been idle. After landing his men, with his two hundred ships he set sail northward, never doubting that his army would sweep all before it. A typhoon carried his fleet far south into the China Sea, but he steered again for Luzon and three weeks later was in sight of Corregidor Island.

He sailed down Manila Bay and drew up his fleet in front of the villages on the Pasig River, the present site of Manila. On the shore the people gathered in terror, for all the warriors had gone to fight the invading army, and only old men and women and children remained in the villages.

Hastily they called a council and finally decided to send a messenger out to the

Moro chief with all the gold and things of value they possessed, thinking thus to satisfy the fierce Datto and save their villages from harm.

Accordingly the women gave their rings and bracelets and the men their bangles and chains. Everything of value was taken from the houses. Even the temples of prayer were stripped and all the ornaments taken. So great was the fear of the people that they even sent the gold statue of the great god Captan that was the pride of the tribe, whose members came miles to worship it.

As Bungtao was preparing to land and attack the town with his sailors, the messenger in his canoe came alongside the ship and was at once taken before the Datto. Trembling with fear, the old man, with signs, begged for mercy for the people on the shore. He pointed to the presents and offered them to Bungtao. Then, placing the golden image of Captan at the feet of the Moro and bowing low, he again pleaded for the women and children.

Bungtao laughed in scorn at the offer. On his island was gold enough to satisfy his people. He needed slaves to work in the fields, for it was beneath the dignity of such warriors as himself and his companions to labor. So he kicked the messenger from him and, with a curse, picked up the sacred golden image and threw it far over the water. Instantly the sky grew dark and blackest night covered the land. The messenger felt himself seized by invisible hands and carried to the shore.

Then suddenly the heavens opened, and a shower of silver fire rained on the Moro boats. In vain the Moros tried to escape. The fire hemmed them in on every side. Many leaped from the burning ships into the boiling water. When the darkness cleared, boats and Moros had disappeared.

Joyfully the people on the shore ran to the temple of worship to pray to Captan. What was their surprise to find the golden image of the god in its usual place, and around it the bracelets and rings offered to the Moros!

When the warriors, a few days later, returned from their great victory in the south, they could hardly believe the story of the wonderful escape of their people. But at night, when they saw the heretofore dull waters dashing and breaking on the shore in crystals of silvery light, they knew that it was Captan who had saved their homes and families.

The villages are a thing of the past. The modern city of Manila now stands on the banks of the Pasig.

The nights here are very beautiful. The breeze sighs softly through the palm trees and the golden moon gleams on the waters of Manila Bay.

On the shore the waves break gently and little balls of silver light go rushing up the beach. Wise men say that the water is full of phosphorus. But they have never heard the story of the Silver Shower.

The Faithlessness of Sinogo

Somewhere off the northern coast of Mindanao a strong current begins to travel northward. It runs to the island of Siquijor and then, turning slightly to the east, goes racing between the islands of Cebu and Negros. At the narrow entrance between San Sebastian and Ayucatan it breaks up into hundreds of small whirlpools that make the water hiss and bubble for a distance of nearly three miles.

For steamers and large boats there is not the slightest danger, but to the native in his little sacayan with its bamboo outriggers these whirlpools are objects of dread and fear. He will go miles out of his way to escape them. If you inquire as to the reason, he will explain that the Liloan, or whirlpool, is a thing always to be avoided, and then he will tell you the story of Sinogo.

Years and years ago, when Maguayan ruled the sea and the terrible Captan launched his thunderbolts from above, the water and air were filled with swimming and flying monsters. Those that lived in the air were armed with great teeth and sharp claws; but, though they were fierce and savage, they lived together in peace, for they feared the anger of their master Captan.

In the sea, however, all was not so peaceful, for some of the monsters were so huge and savage and so confident in their strength that Maguayan could do nothing with them. He lived in constant fear of attack from these fierce subjects and finally, in despair, called on Captan to help him in his trouble.

Accordingly Captan sent his swift messengers to every part of the earth, air, and sea, and ordered that a council of all the creatures in the world should be held. He named the little island of Caueli in the center of the Sulu Sea as the meeting place, and commanded all to hasten there without delay.

Soon the members of the council began to arrive, and the sky was darkened by flying monsters, and the water boiled as the terrible reptiles of the sea rushed to the place appointed.

In a short time the little island was crowded with these dreadful creatures. There were huge Buayas from Mindanao, fierce Tic-bolans from Luzon, savage Sigbins from Negros and Bohol, hundreds of Unglocs from Panay and Leyte, and great Uak Uaks and other frightful monsters from Samar and Cebu. They grouped themselves in a large circle around a golden throne on which sat Captan and Maguayan, and while waiting the commands of their master filled the air with shrieks and howls.

At length Captan raised his hand and the noise instantly stopped. Then he announced his decree. He said that Maguayan was his brother god and should be treated with the same respect. He commanded all his subjects to obey the god of the sea and told them that he would kill with a thunderbolt any that disobeyed this order. Then he desired all to return to their own regions, and again the air was filled with a noise of thunder and the sea roared and foamed as the monsters went back to their homes.

Soon there remained on the island only Captan, Maguayan, and three messengers of Captan, who were called Sinogo, Dalagan, and Guidala. These were giants in size and had large wings which enabled them to fly with great swiftness. They had long spears and sharp swords and were very brave and powerful. Of the three, Dalagan was the swiftest, Guidala the bravest, and Sinogo the handsomest and best loved by Captan.

When all the creatures were gone Maguayan thanked Captan, but the great god said that he had only done his duty in helping his brother. Then he gave Maguayan a little golden shell and explained to him its wonderful power. Maguayan had but to put it in his mouth and he could change his form to that of any creature he pleased. In case a monster, defying Captan's orders, should attack him, he had simply to change himself into a stronger monster of twice the size of his enemy, and then fight and kill him easily.

Again Maguayan thanked his brother god and, taking the shell, placed it on the throne beside him. Then Captan ordered his messengers to bring food and drink, and soon the two gods were feasting merrily.

Now it happened that Sinogo had been standing behind the throne and had heard all that had been said. He was filled with a desire to own the wonderful shell, and in spite of the many favors he had received from Captan he resolved to steal it. The more he thought of its great power, the more he longed for it. With it he could rule the earth and sea as a god, and, by hiding, he might avoid the anger of Captan. So he watched for an opportunity to make away with it. Finally his chance came. While handing Maguayan some food, he slyly caught up the shell, and soon afterwards quietly slipped away.

For some time his absence was not discovered, but all at once Captan called for his favorite messenger and, receiving no reply, ordered Dalagan to search for him. Soon Dalagan returned and reported that Sinogo could not be found on the island. At the same time Maguayan noticed that the golden shell was gone.

Then Captan knew that his messenger had stolen the shell and escaped. He flew into a great rage and swore he would kill Sinogo. He ordered Dalagan and Guidala to hasten to the north in search of the faithless messenger and to bring him back a prisoner.

Swiftly northward over the blue sea flew the messengers, and near the island of Guimaras caught sight of Sinogo. He saw his pursuers and flew all the swifter, but he was no match for them in speed. Nearer and nearer they came and then, drawing their swords, rushed forward to seize him.

But Sinogo was not to be easily caught. Quick as a flash, he placed the shell in his mouth and dived down into the water, at the same time changing himself into a huge crocodile-shaped Buaya with scales like armor of steel.

In vain Dalagan and Guidala rained blows on the monster. The swords could not pierce the heavy scales.

Up through Guimaras Strait the chase went on, and Sinogo tore up the water in his flight. So great was the disturbance of the ocean that, as they rounded the northern coast of Negros, the waves dashed completely over the little island of Bacabac, sweeping away the hills and bringing the land to the level of the sea.

Still the rapid flight went on. Straight for Bantayan headed Sinogo, but suddenly changing his course he dashed into the narrow channel between Negros and Cebu. Then Dalagan, leaving Guidala to continue the chase alone, flew swiftly back to Caueli and told Captan that Sinogo was in the little strait. Up sprang the god and, flying directly east, he posted himself at the southern entrance of the channel. In his hand he held an enormous thunderbolt, and thus armed he waited for the appearance of Sinogo.

Down into the narrow entrance sped the faithless messenger, tearing up the water in his mad flight, while the brave Guidala struck in vain at his huge body. Suddenly a roar of thunder sounded and the thunderbolt fell on the back of the monster, bearing him down beneath the waves and then, stiffening like a bar of iron, pinning him to the bottom far below. In vain he struggled to free himself; the bar held him fast and sure. In his struggles the shell fell from his mouth, but a little Tamban caught it and brought it safely to Captan.

Thousands of years have passed, but far under the water, like a fly on a pin, Sinogo struggles in the form of a huge Buaya. The water bubbles around him and for three miles little whirlpools go racing up the channel. And the native in his little sacayan avoids the narrow entrance where the water boils and foams, for Sinogo still twists and squirms, and the Liloan is a thing to be feared and dreaded.

Catalina of Dumaguete

This is a legend of Dumaguete, the capital of the province of Negros Occidental. From this town can be seen five islands, viz., Negros, Cebu, Bohol, Mindanao, and Siquijor.

There is no one on the great island of Negros who does not love the name of Catalina. Even the wild mountain men speak it with respect, and down in the coast towns at night, when the typhoon is lashing the waters of Tanon Strait, and the rain and wind make the nipa leaves on the roofs dance and rattle, the older people gather their little black-eyed grandchildren around the shell of burning cocoanut oil and tell them her story.

Many years ago there lived in Dumaguete a poor tuba seller named Banog, who made his daily rounds to the houses just as the milkman does in far-off America. But instead of a rattling wagon he had only a long bamboo from which he poured the drink, and in place of sweet milk he left the sap of the cocoanut tree.

The bad custom of mixing tungud, a kind of red bark, with the sap, and thus making of it a strong liquor, had not yet been known, so Banog, though poor, was respected, and the people tried in every way to help him and his daughter Catalina.

Catalina was a beautiful girl of sixteen and very good and industrious, but with many strange ways. She scarcely ever spoke a word and spent most of her time in looking out over the sea. Sometimes she would suddenly stand erect and, clasping her hands, would remain for a long time looking up at the sky as if she saw something that no one else could see. On account of these strange manners the people thought her a wonderful girl and she was supposed to have mysterious powers.

One day many ships came up from the island of Mindanao and hundreds of fierce Moros landed. Shouting and waving their terrible knives, they fell upon the peaceful people and killed many, among them poor Banog. Then they robbed and burned the houses and, seizing all the women they could find, set sail for their great southern island. Among the prisoners was Catalina. With her eyes fixed on the sky she sat very quiet and still in the bow of one of the boats, and though her companions spoke often to her she made no reply.

Suddenly she sprang into the water and a wonderful thing occurred, for, instead of sinking, she walked lightly over the waves toward the distant shore. The Moros were so astonished that they did not try to stop her and she reached the land safely.

Many people who had hidden in the forests ran out to meet her but she spoke to no one. With her eyes still fixed above she walked through the burning town and along the road to Dalugdug, the Thunder mountain, that lies behind Dumaguete.

On Dalugdug there lived a terrible Sigbin. Its body was like that of a monstrous crow, but just under its neck were two long legs like those of a grasshopper, which enabled it to leap great distances without using its wings. It ate any one who came near its home, so when the people saw Catalina start to climb the mountain they begged her to come back. She paid no heed to their cries, however, but went up higher and higher, till her white dress seemed merely a speck on the mountain side.

All at once she seemed to stop and raise her hands. Then a fearful shriek was heard, and the fierce Sigbin came rushing down the mountain. It appeared to be greatly frightened, for it took tremendous leaps and screamed as if in terror. Over the heads of the people it jumped, and, reaching the shore, cleared the narrow channel and disappeared among the mountains of the island of Cebu.

When the people saw that the Sigbin had gone they ran up the mountain and searched everywhere for Catalina, but they could find no trace of her. Sorrowfully they returned to their homes and busied themselves in building new houses and in making their town beautiful once more.

Several years passed in peace and then again the Moro boats came up from Mindanao. The men hurriedly gathered on the beach to meet them, and the women and children hid in the cocoanut groves.

This time the Moros had no quick and easy victory, for the Visayans, armed with bolos and remembering their lost wives and sisters, fought furiously, and for a time drove the enemy before them. But more Moro boats arrived and numbers told against the defenders. Slowly but surely they fell fighting until but a few remained.

Suddenly a bridge of clouds unfolded from Dalugdug to the town, and across it came the lost Catalina holding a beehive in her hands. Then she spoke and thousands of bees flew from the hive to the ground. Again she spoke and waved her hand, and the bees changed into little black men with long sharp spears, who charged the Moros and killed every one of them.

Then Catalina, the hive still in her hand, went back over the bridge and disappeared once more in the mountain.

The people came out of their hiding places, crowding around the little black men and questioning them, but they received no answer. Instead the little warriors gathered together and ran into the forest and up the mountain side, where they were soon lost to view.

Such is the story of Catalina, Since that time Dumaguete has been safe from the Moros. The Sigbin has never returned to Negros. It still lives in the mountains of Cebu and the people are so afraid of it that they lock themselves in their houses after dark and can hardly be induced to come out. Up in the mountains of Negros live the little black men. They are called Negritos and are very savage and wild.

The savior of Dumaguete still lives in Dalugdug and is worshiped by the people. And in the town, now grown into a big busy city, the old people for years to come will tell their grandchildren the story of Catalina.

The Fall of Polobulac

This is a tale from Panay. It probably originated with the Spanish fathers, who wished to impress the doctrine of the Seven Deadly Sins on the natives. The islands are just off Iloilo.

A little way from Iloilo there once was a beautiful island called Polobulac, or Isle of Flowers. Its shores were covered with beautiful trees and plants; splendid gardens of flowers were found everywhere; fruits grew in abundance; fountains sparkled in the sunlight; and the people were the happiest in the world. They danced and sang to gay music, and were free from every care and sorrow.

Filled with confidence in their good fortune, and proud of their beautiful island, they began to slight the people of the neighboring islands, and to treat them with insolence and scorn.

One night the sky was darkened, the lightning flashed, the rain fell in torrents, and a voice cried from the clouds, above the roar of the thunder:

"I am Pride. Avoid me or perish."

Terrified, they prayed to God for protection, but with the morning sun their fears left them and they continued as before.

Days passed and the people grew richer, but, not satisfied with their wealth and with their own beautiful island, they longed to possess the lands of their neighbors.

Again came the storm, and again a voice cried from the heavens:

"I am Covetousness. Come to me and die."

Once more they appealed for protection, but they did not change their ways.

Weeks went by, and with wealth came low and base desires. The storm came as before and brought the warning:

"I am Evil Desire. Fly from me or be lost."

But again it sounded to sealed ears. Months rolled on. The people quarreled with their neighbors, and sent forth an army to make war upon them. The voice thundered:

"I am Anger. I give eternal torment."

Years followed, and the tables of the people of Polobulac were loaded with the finest foods and wines. Day and night found them feasting. The cry sounded above them:

"I am Gluttony. I devour my children."

The winds alone echoed the warning.

Time flew by. Each man sought to outdo the others in display of luxury and magnificence. The poor grudged the rich their fortunes, and sought in every way to injure them. Again a voice came through the darkness:

"I am Envy. My people are condemned."

But they closed their ears and would not hear.

More wealth brought greater luxury. They lolled in idleness. They idled in the midst of magnificence. The voice warned:

"I am Sloth. I bring final warning."

They were used to the voices now, and gave them not the slightest heed. Their insolence and greed grew greater. The fair island shook with dissension and strife.

One day the sun was hidden by blackness. A fearful tempest burst over the land. The people on the other islands saw Polobulac wrapped in seven huge pillars of flame.

When the sky cleared, Polobulac was nowhere to be seen. In its place, seven blackened rocks marked the spot where stood the beautiful isle.

They are there to this day. You can see them as you leave the harbor for southern ports. Sometimes they appear as one. Again they seem to group in twos and threes. But there are seven.

They are called the Deadly Sins.

The Escape of Juanita

Have you heard of the terrible Tic-balan, A tall and thin and very black man, With terrible teeth and a horse's head, And covered with hair that is long and red?

He lives in the awful Balete tree, And to pass the place you must say "Tabi"; If you do not, the Asuang comes at night, And throws big stones till you die of fright.

Now once there lived in Santa Cruz town A little girl known as Juanita Calaon; She was gentle and sweet and as good as could be, And she always bowed low to the Balete tree.

One day to the forest alone she did roam To get some good wood for the fire at home; She gathered some twigs that she found on the ground, And all of them fast in a bundle she bound.

Then happy and free, with the pack on her head, She followed the road that back to town led. She sang as she walked, and so happy was she That alas! she bowed not to the Balete tree.

All at once then she heard a most terrible roar, And the Tic-balan fierce through the air seemed to soar. He seized poor Juanita, and quick as could be He shut her inside of the Balete tree.

Two days passed, and when the girl failed to come back, Her parents went out, and no friends did they lack To help in the search, for the whole pueblo came, And loudly they shouted poor Juanita's name.

At last when they thought that the search brought no good, One man found Juanita's neat bundle of wood; He called the good news, and as more came to see, Loud knocking was heard in the Balete tree.

Then many were frightened, but many were brave, And wondered by what means the girl they could save; For they knew that it must be Juanita who knocked, And that inside the Balete tree she was locked.

Soon they ordered that candles and music be brought, And a crucifix holy was what they next sought; And when all was ready they closed round the tree, While they prayed to the true God to set the girl free.

They lighted the candles and then the band played, And Juanita's mother, who was not afraid, Advanced with the crucifix held in her hand, And tapped with the cross on the evil tree grand.

Then a roar shook the forest and chilled all their hearts, And the awful Balete split into two parts; Then they saw in the center, as each big half fell, Their darling Juanita all smiling and well.

She ran from the tree to her fond mother dear, While the band played and every one gave a loud cheer; Then back to the pueblo they danced in delight, And kept up their singing through all the long night.

Still there to this day lies the Balete tree, But no more do the people that pass say "Tabi." And the spirit no more can molest any man, For God has more power than the fierce Tic-balan.

The Anting-Anting of Manuelito

The Anting-Anting is a stone or other small object covered with cabalistic inscriptions. It is worn around the neck, and is supposed to render its owner impervious to knife or bullet. Many are wearing these charms, especially the Tulisanes or outlaws. The Anting-Anting must not be confused, however, with the scapular, a purely religious symbol worn by a great number of the Christian Filipinos.

Many of the older Filipinos remember Manuelito, the great Tulisane, who, more than fifty years ago, kept all the Laguna de Bai district in a state of fear. His robber band was well organized and obeyed his slightest wish. He had many boats on the lake and many hiding places in the mountains, and throughout the country there was no villager who did not fear to oppose him, or who would refuse to help him in any way when required to do so.

In vain the Guardia Civil hunted him. Many times they surrounded the band, but Manuelito always escaped. Many shots were fired at him, but he was never hit; and once, when he was cut off from his men and surrounded, he broke through the line, and though fifty bullets whistled around him he did not receive a scratch.

The officers of the Guardia Civil blamed their men for the bad marksmanship that allowed Manuelito to escape. They told all the people that it should never occur again, and promised that the next fight should end in the death of the outlaw. The people, however, did not believe that Manuelito could be killed, for he wore on his breast a famous Anting-Anting that he had received from Mangagauay, the giver of life and death.

This charm was a stone covered with mysterious signs. It was wrapped in silk and hung by a string from the robber's neck, and even if a gun were fired within a few feet of him the Anting-Anting was sure to turn the bullet in another direction.

It was this charm that always saved him from the Guardia Civil.

Manuelito was very proud of his Anting-Anting, and many times, when a fiesta was being held in some town, he and his band would come down from the mountains and take part in the games. Manuelito would stand in the town plaza and allow his men to shoot at him, and each time the Anting-Anting would turn aside the bullets. The people were very much impressed, and though a few of the wiser ones secretly thought that the guns were only loaded with powder, they were afraid to say anything; so the greater number thought it very wonderful and believed that there was no charm so powerful as the Anting-Anting of Manuelito.

For years the Tulisane, protected by his charm, continued to rob and plunder. The Guardia Civil hunted him everywhere, but could never kill him. He grew bolder and bolder, and even came close to Manila to rob the little towns just outside the city.

At last the government grew tired of sending out the Guardia Civil, and ordered a regiment of Macabebes to hunt and kill the Tulisane and his men.

Manuelito was at Pasay when news was brought to him that the Macabebes were coming. Instead of running from these fierce little fighters, he decided to meet them, and many people offered to help him, believing that the Anting-Anting would turn away all bullets and give them victory. So Manuelito and many men left the town, built trenches in the hills near San Pedro Macati, and waited for the Macabebes to appear.

They had not long to wait. The Macabebes, hurrying from Manila, reached San Pedro Macati and soon found that Manuelito was waiting to fight them. They left the town at once and advanced on the Tulisane trenches.

It was a great fight. From the other hills close by many people watched the battle. Five times the Macabebes advanced, and were forced to fall back before the fierce fire of the Tulisanes. But the Macabebe never knows defeat, and once more their line went forward and in one terrible charge swept over the trenches and bayoneted the outlaws. In vain Manuelito called on his men to fight. They broke and ran in every direction. Then, seeing that all was lost, Manuelito started to follow them; but a volley rang out, and, struck by twenty bullets, he fell to the ground dead. The Macabebes chased the flying Tulisanes and killed that of all the band only a few many, safely reached the mountains.

While the Macabebes were chasing the outlaws, many people came down from the hills and stood around the body of Manuelito. They could hardly believe their eyes, but the many wounds and the blood staining the ground proved that the great Tulisane was indeed dead.

What of the Anting-Anting? Had it lost its power?

One man timidly unbuttoned the shirt of the dead robber and pulled out the charm. The mystery was explained. Fixed firmly in the center of the Anting-Anting was a silver bullet. There was but one explanation. The Macabebes had melted a statue of the Virgin and used it to make bullets to fire at Manuelito. Against such bullets the charm was useless, but against ordinary lead it never would have failed. Had not the people seen Manuelito's own men fire at him?

The charm was taken from the neck of the dead Tulisane and many copies were made of it. Even to this day hundreds of people are wearing them. They will tell you about Manuelito's great fight and also about his famous Anting-Anting.

"But," you say, "the Anting-Anting was useless. Manuelito was killed."

They answer, "Yes, Senor, it is true; but the Macabebes used bullets of silver. Had they used lead the story would have been different. Poor Manuelito!"

When the Lilies Return

Alegend of the Chinese Invasion. Quiapo, even at the time of the early Spaniards, and for years after, was a deserted field. The story is an old one and generally known to the Tagallos.

At the time when the Pasig flowed peacefully along between flowery banks; when its breast was not torn by puffing steamers; and when only a few clustering huts marked the present site of Manila, there grew on the banks of the river a beautiful field of lilies.

The lilies glistened like silver in the sunlight, and their sweet odor filled the air with delicious perfume. No hand plucked them from the earth, and no foot trampled out their fragrance; for an ancient prophecy had said that while the lilies stood the happiness of the people should endure.

But after a time there came dark days in the history of the Philippines. Yellow hordes swept across the water and carried all before them. The people could hardly expect to resist the invaders, for their warrior king, Loku, had profaned the word of the god, and, in the form of a lizard, was fulfilling his punishment. Their armies were weak and scattered, and the conquerors marched on in triumph.

As report after report of disaster reached Luzon, the people trembled for the safety of their fair land. Warriors gathered hastily for the defense of the nation, and all waited for the enemy to appear.

One day the water was dotted with the junks of the invaders. They came slowly down the bay, and anchored near the mouth of the Pasig.

Then from the boats poured the yellow warriors. Spears rained upon them, stones and arrows laid them low, but their numbers were countless. The people were swept back along the river banks.

Fiercely they fought, but numbers told against them. Foot by foot they were pressed back, till they stood on the border of the field of lilies, where they made their last stand. But it was to no purpose.

The invaders poured from the ships, and in one desperate charge drove back the ranks of the people, who fought and died among their sacred lilies.

All through the night the battle raged, and at daybreak, when the victorious invaders rested on their spears, the beautiful field was no more.

The lilies were crushed and torn. The bodies of dead and dying warriors lay everywhere, and the crushed flowers were stained with the blood of friend and foe. The peace of the land was lost.

Many years have passed since then. New races have come to the Islands, and new manners and customs have been introduced. The Pasig still flows on to the sea, but its banks are harnessed by bridges. Lofty dwellings and stores take the place of the little huts, and a great city marks the site of the little village.

Where once was the beautiful field is now a busy part of the great city. It is called Quiapo, after the lilies. Many of the older people remember the prophecy and wonder if the lilies will ever return.

The land is now a peaceful and contented one. Comfort and happiness may be found among its inhabitants. Perhaps the fair, strange women from the great land over the sea are the lilies. Who can tell?

Glossary

balete tree = a type of tree, Ficus indica, often believed to be the home of evil and vengeful spirits. camisas = shirts. chinela = slipper. cocheros = drivers of horse-drawn carriages. Datto = chief. Guardia Civil = Spanish police. ladrones = thieves. lubi lana = coconut oil. Moro = Muslim's from the southern islands of the Philippines. Negritos = Negroid people indigenous in some parts of the Philippines. nipa = palm leaf of which the roofs of cheap houses are made. sacayan = small outrigger boat. tuba = alcoholic drink made from the sap of the coconut tree. tungud = the red bark of a mangrove tree.

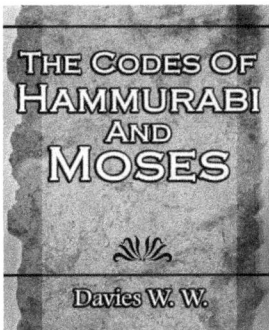

The Codes Of Hammurabi And Moses
W. W. Davies

QTY

The discovery of the Hammurabi Code is one of the greatest achievements of archaeology, and is of paramount interest, not only to the student of the Bible, but also to all those interested in ancient history...

Religion   ISBN: *1-59462-338-4*   **Pages:132**
MSRP $12.95

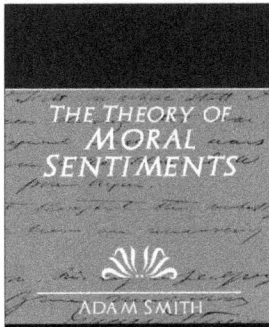

The Theory of Moral Sentiments
Adam Smith

QTY

This work from 1749. contains original theories of conscience amd moral judgment and it is the foundation for systemof morals.

Philosophy ISBN: *1-59462-777-0*   **Pages:536**
MSRP $19.95

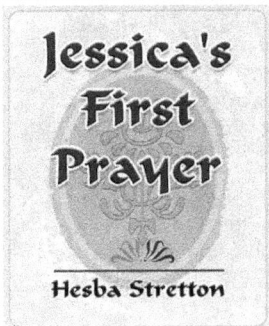

Jessica's First Prayer
Hesba Stretton

QTY

In a screened and secluded corner of one of the many railway-bridges which span the streets of London there could be seen a few years ago, from five o'clock every morning until half past eight, a tidily set-out coffee-stall, consisting of a trestle and board, upon which stood two large tin cans, with a small fire of charcoal burning under each so as to keep the coffee boiling during the early hours of the morning when the work-people were thronging into the city on their way to their daily toil...

Childrens   ISBN: *1-59462-373-2*   **Pages:84**
MSRP $9.95

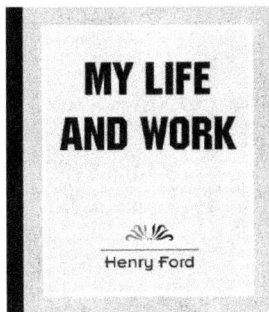

My Life and Work
Henry Ford

QTY

Henry Ford revolutionized the world with his implementation of mass production for the Model T automobile. Gain valuable business insight into his life and work with his own auto-biography... "We have only started on our development of our country we have not as yet, with all our talk of wonderful progress, done more than scratch the surface. The progress has been wonderful enough but..."

Biographies/   ISBN: *1-59462-198-5*   **Pages:300**
MSRP $21.95

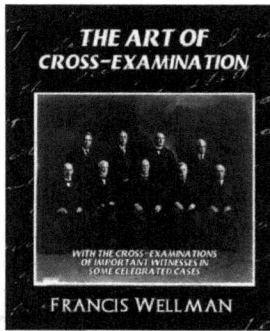

The Art of Cross-Examination
Francis Wellman

QTY

I presume it is the experience of every author, after his first book is published upon an important subject, to be almost overwhelmed with a wealth of ideas and illustrations which could readily have been included in his book, and which to his own mind, at least, seem to make a second edition inevitable. Such certainly was the case with me; and when the first edition had reached its sixth impression in five months, I rejoiced to learn that it seemed to my publishers that the book had met with a sufficiently favorable reception to justify a second and considerably enlarged edition. ..

Reference   ISBN: *1-59462-647-2*

Pages:412
MSRP $19.95

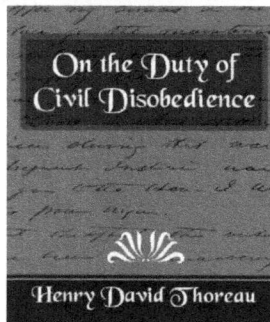

On the Duty of Civil Disobedience
Henry David Thoreau

QTY

Thoreau wrote his famous essay, On the Duty of Civil Disobedience, as a protest against an unjust but popular war and the immoral but popular institution of slave-owning. He did more than write—he declined to pay his taxes, and was hauled off to gaol in consequence. Who can say how much this refusal of his hastened the end of the war and of slavery ?

Law   ISBN: *1-59462-747-9*

Pages:48
MSRP $7.45

Dream Psychology Psychoanalysis for Beginners
Sigmund Freud

QTY

Sigmund Freud, born Sigismund Schlomo Freud (May 6, 1856 - September 23, 1939), was a Jewish-Austrian neurologist and psychiatrist who co-founded the psychoanalytic school of psychology. Freud is best known for his theories of the unconscious mind, especially involving the mechanism of repression; his redefinition of sexual desire as mobile and directed towards a wide variety of objects; and his therapeutic techniques, especially his understanding of transference in the therapeutic relationship and the presumed value of dreams as sources of insight into unconscious desires.

Psychology   ISBN: *1-59462-905-6*

Pages:196
MSRP $15.45

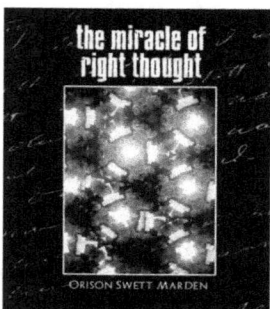

The Miracle of Right Thought
Orison Swett Marden

QTY

Believe with all of your heart that you will do what you were made to do. When the mind has once formed the habit of holding cheerful, happy, prosperous pictures, it will not be easy to form the opposite habit. It does not matter how improbable or how far away this realization may see, or how dark the prospects may be, if we visualize them as best we can, as vividly as possible, hold tenaciously to them and vigorously struggle to attain them, they will gradually become actualized, realized in the life. But a desire, a longing without endeavor, a yearning abandoned or held indifferently will vanish without realization.

Self Help   ISBN: *1-59462-644-8*

Pages:360
MSRP $25.45

QTY

The Rosicrucian Cosmo-Conception Mystic Christianity *by Max Heindel*   ISBN: *1-59462-188-8*   **$38.95**
The Rosicrucian Cosmo-conception is not dogmatic, neither does it appeal to any other authority than the reason of the student. It is: not controversial, but is: sent forth in the, hope that it may help to clear...   New Age/Religion Pages 646

Abandonment To Divine Providence *by Jean-Pierre de Caussade*   ISBN: *1-59462-228-0*   **$25.95**
"The Rev. Jean Pierre de Caussade was one of the most remarkable spiritual writers of the Society of Jesus in France in the 18th Century. His death took place at Toulouse in 1751. His works have gone through many editions and have been republished...   Inspirational/Religion Pages 400

Mental Chemistry *by Charles Haanel*   ISBN: *1-59462-192-6*   **$23.95**
Mental Chemistry allows the change of material conditions by combining and appropriately utilizing the power of the mind. Much like applied chemistry creates something new and unique out of careful combinations of chemicals the mastery of mental chemistry...   New Age Pages 354

The Letters of Robert Browning and Elizabeth Barret Barrett 1845-1846 vol II   ISBN: *1-59462-193-4*   **$35.95**
by Robert Browning and Elizabeth Barrett   Biographies Pages 596

Gleanings In Genesis (volume I) *by Arthur W. Pink*   ISBN: *1-59462-130-6*   **$27.45**
Appropriately has Genesis been termed "the seed plot of the Bible" for in it we have, in germ form, almost all of the great doctrines which are afterwards fully developed in the books of Scripture which follow...   Religion/Inspirational Pages 420

The Master Key *by L. W. de Laurence*   ISBN: *1-59462-001-6*   **$30.95**
In no branch of human knowledge has there been a more lively increase of the spirit of research during the past few years than in the study of Psychology, Concentration and Mental Discipline. The requests for authentic lessons in Thought Control, Mental Discipline and...   New Age/Business Pages 422

The Lesser Key Of Solomon Goetia *by L. W. de Laurence*   ISBN: *1-59462-092-X*   **$9.95**
This translation of the first book of the "Lernegton" which is now for the first time made accessible to students of Talismanic Magic was done, after careful collation and edition, from numerous Ancient Manuscripts in Hebrew, Latin, and French...   New Age/Occult Pages 92

Rubaiyat Of Omar Khayyam *by Edward Fitzgerald*   ISBN:*1-59462-332-5*   **$13.95**
Edward Fitzgerald, whom the world has already learned, in spite of his own efforts to remain within the shadow of anonymity, to look upon as one of the rarest poets of the century, was born at Bredfield, in Suffolk, on the 31st of March, 1809. He was the third son of John Purcell...   Music Pages 172

Ancient Law *by Henry Maine*   ISBN: *1-59462-128-4*   **$29.95**
The chief object of the following pages is to indicate some of the earliest ideas of mankind, as they are reflected in Ancient Law, and to point out the relation of those ideas to modern thought.   Religion/History Pages 452

Far-Away Stories *by William J. Locke*   ISBN: *1-59462-129-2*   **$19.45**
"Good wine needs no bush, but a collection of mixed vintages does. And this book is just such a collection. Some of the stories I do not want to remain buried for ever in the museum files of dead magazine-numbers an author's not unpardonable vanity..."   Fiction Pages 272

Life of David Crockett *by David Crockett*   ISBN: *1-59462-250-7*   **$27.45**
"Colonel David Crockett was one of the most remarkable men of the times in which he lived. Born in humble life, but gifted with a strong will, an indomitable courage, and unremitting perseverance...   Biographies/New Age Pages 424

Lip-Reading *by Edward Nitchie*   ISBN: *1-59462-206-X*   **$25.95**
Edward B. Nitchie, founder of the New York School for the Hard of Hearing, now the Nitchie School of Lip-Reading, Inc, wrote "LIP-READING Principles and Practice". The development and perfecting of this meritorious work on lip-reading was an undertaking...   How-to Pages 400

A Handbook of Suggestive Therapeutics, Applied Hypnotism, Psychic Science   ISBN: *1-59462-214-0*   **$24.95**
by Henry Munro   Health/New Age/Health/Self-help Pages 376

A Doll's House: and Two Other Plays *by Henrik Ibsen*   ISBN: *1-59462-112-8*   **$19.95**
Henrik Ibsen created this classic when in revolutionary 1848 Rome. Introducing some striking concepts in playwriting for the realist genre, this play has been studied the world over.   Fiction/Classics/Plays 308

The Light of Asia *by sir Edwin Arnold*   ISBN: *1-59462-204-3*   **$13.95**
In this poetic masterpiece, Edwin Arnold describes the life and teachings of Buddha. The man who was to become known as Buddha to the world was born as Prince Gautama of India but he rejected the worldly riches and abandoned the reigns of power when...   Religion/History/Biographies Pages 170

The Complete Works of Guy de Maupassant *by Guy de Maupassant*   ISBN: *1-59462-157-8*   **$16.95**
"For days and days, nights and nights, I had dreamed of that first kiss which was to consecrate our engagement, and I knew not on what spot I should put my lips..."   Fiction/Classics Pages 240

The Art of Cross-Examination *by Francis L. Wellman*   ISBN: *1-59462-309-0*   **$26.95**
Written by a renowned trial lawyer, Wellman imparts his experience and uses case studies to explain how to use psychology to extract desired information through questioning.   How-to/Science/Reference Pages 408

Answered or Unanswered? *by Louisa Vaughan*   ISBN: *1-59462-248-5*   **$10.95**
Miracles of Faith in China   Religion Pages 112

The Edinburgh Lectures on Mental Science (1909) *by Thomas*   ISBN: *1-59462-008-3*   **$11.95**
This book contains the substance of a course of lectures recently given by the writer in the Queen Street Hall, Edinburgh. Its purpose is to indicate the Natural Principles governing the relation between Mental Action and Material Conditions...   New Age/Psychology Pages 148

Ayesha *by H. Rider Haggard*   ISBN: *1-59462-301-5*   **$24.95**
Verily and indeed it is the unexpected that happens! Probably if there was one person upon the earth from whom the Editor of this, and of a certain previous history, did not expect to hear again...   Classics Pages 380

Ayala's Angel *by Anthony Trollope*   ISBN: *1-59462-352-X*   **$29.95**
The two girls were both pretty, but Lucy who was twenty-one who supposed to be simple and comparatively unattractive, whereas Ayala was credited, as her Bombwhat romantic name might show, with poetic charm and a taste for romance. Ayala when her father died was nineteen...   Fiction Pages 484

The American Commonwealth *by James Bryce*   ISBN: *1-59462-286-8*   **$34.45**
An interpretation of American democratic political theory. It examines political mechanics and society from the perspective of Scotsman James Bryce   Politics Pages 572

Stories of the Pilgrims *by Margaret P. Pumphrey*   ISBN: *1-59462-116-0*   **$17.95**
This book explores pilgrims religious oppression in England as well as their escape to Holland and eventual crossing to America on the Mayflower, and their early days in New England...   History Pages 268

QTY

The Fasting Cure *by Sinclair Upton* ISBN: *1-59462-222-1* **$13.95**

In the Cosmopolitan Magazine for May, 1910, and in the Contemporary Review (London) for April, 1910, I published an article dealing with my experiences in fasting. I have written a great many magazine articles, but never one which attracted so much attention... New Age/Self Help/Health Pages 164

Hebrew Astrology *by Sepharial* ISBN: *1-59462-308-2* **$13.45**

In these days of advanced thinking it is a matter of common observation that we have left many of the old landmarks behind and that we are now pressing forward to greater heights and to a wider horizon than that which represented the mind-content of our progenitors... Astrology Pages 144

Thought Vibration or The Law of Attraction in the Thought World ISBN: *1-59462-127-6* **$12.95**

by William Walker Atkinson Psychology/Religion Pages 144

Optimism *by Helen Keller* ISBN: *1-59462-108-X* **$15.95**

Helen Keller was blind, deaf, and mute since 19 months old, yet famously learned how to overcome these handicaps, communicate with the world, and spread her lectures promoting optimism. An inspiring read for everyone... Biographies/Inspirational Pages 84

Sara Crewe *by Frances Burnett* ISBN: *1-59462-360-0* **$9.45**

In the first place, Miss Minchin lived in London. Her home was a large, dull, tall one, in a large, dull square, where all the houses were alike, and all the sparrows were alike, and where all the door-knockers made the same heavy sound... Childrens/Classic Pages 88

The Autobiography of Benjamin Franklin *by Benjamin Franklin* ISBN: *1-59462-135-7* **$24.95**

The Autobiography of Benjamin Franklin has probably been more extensively read than any other American historical work, and no other book of its kind has had such ups and downs of fortune. Franklin lived for many years in England, where he was agent... Biographies/History Pages 332

Name	
Email	
Telephone	
Address	
City, State ZIP	

☐ **Credit Card**   ☐ **Check / Money Order**

Credit Card Number	
Expiration Date	
Signature	

Please Mail to: Book Jungle
PO Box 2226
Champaign, IL 61825
or Fax to: 630-214-0564

ORDERING INFORMATION

web*: www.bookjungle.com*
email*: sales@bookjungle.com*
fax*: 630-214-0564*
mail*: Book Jungle PO Box 2226 Champaign, IL 61825*
or PayPal *to sales@bookjungle.com*

Please contact us for bulk discounts

DIRECT-ORDER TERMS

**20% Discount if You Order
Two or More Books**
Free Domestic Shipping!
Accepted: Master Card, Visa,
Discover, American Express

www.ingramcontent.com/pod-product-compliance
Lightning Source LLC
Chambersburg PA
CBHW080057280326

41934CB00014B/3342